Plant Top Tens

Europe's Most Amazing Plants

www.raintreepublishers.co.uk
Visit our website to find out more information about Raintree Books.

To order:
☎ Phone 44 (0) 1865 888112
▤ Send a fax to 44 (0) 1865 314091
▣ Visit the Raintree Bookshop at **www.raintreepublishers.co.uk** to browse our catalogue and order online

Raintree is an imprint of Capstone Global Library Limited, a company incorporated in England and Wales having its registered office at 7 Pilgrim Street, London, EC4V 6LB – Registered company number: 6695582

"Raintree" is a registered trademark of Pearson Education Limited, under licence to Capstone Global Library Limited

Text © Capstone Global Library Limited 2008
First published in hardback in 2008
First published in paperback in 2009

Produced for Raintree by Calcium

Editorial: Kate de Villiers and Sarah Eason
Design: Victoria Bevan and Paul Myerscough
Illustrations: Geoff Ward
Picture Research: Maria Joannou
Originated by Modern Age
Printed and bound by China Translation Printing Services

ISBN 978 1 4062 0970 9 (hardback)
12 11 10 09 08
10 9 8 7 6 5 4 3 2 1

ISBN 978 1 4062 0977 8 (paperback)
13 12 11 10 09
10 9 8 7 6 5 4 3 2 1

British Library Cataloguing in Publication Data
Scott, Michael and Royston, Angela
  Europe. - (Plant top tens)
  581.9'4
A full catalogue record for this book is available from the British Library.

Acknowledgements
The authors and publisher are grateful to the following for permission to reproduce copyright material: © Alamy Images pp. 6 (John Ferro Sims), 12 (Swamp Photographic), 14 (Arco Images/De Meester, J), 15 (Arco Images/ Wermter, C), 19 (Glyn Ryland), 20, 21 (blickwinkel); © Corbis p. 9 (Charles O'Rear), 17 (Niall Benvie); © FLPA pp. 8 (Paul Hobson), 23 (Andrew Parkinson); © iStockphoto p. 7; © Nature Picture Library p. 25 (Asgeir Helgestad); © NHPA pp. 18 (Jim Bain), 26 (Martin Garwood); © Photolibrary p. 22 (Oxford Scientific Films); © Rex Features p. 24 (Kaisa Siren); © Science Photo Library p. 13 (Sinclaire Stammers); © Michael Scott p. 16; © Shutterstock pp. 4 (Mikhail Pogosov), 10 (Weldon Schloneger), 12 (Ariel Bravy), 27 (Nikita Tiunov).

Cover photograph of foxgloves reproduced with permission of Ardea/Duncan Usher.

Every effort has been made to contact copyright holders of any material reproduced in this book. Any omissions will be rectified in subsequent printings if notice is given to the publishers.

Contents

Some words are printed in bold, **like this**. You can find out what they mean on page 31 in the Glossary.

Europe

Europe stretches from the **Arctic** Ocean in the north to the Mediterranean Sea in the south. The land just south of the Arctic is frozen all winter and is called **tundra**. Only mosses and other small plants can grow here in summer. The land around the Mediterranean Sea is hot and very dry all summer. Most of the plants that grow here are low bushes, called scrub.

Fewer types of plant grow on these high mountains than on land lower down.

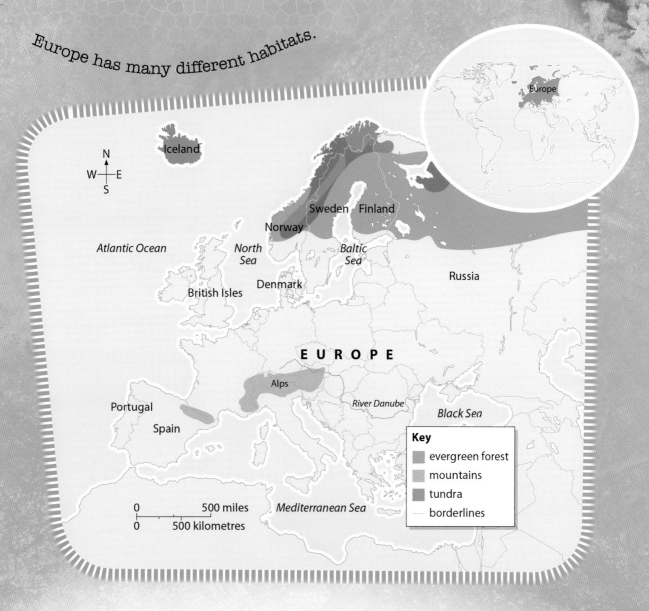

Europe

N
W E
S

Iceland

Atlantic Ocean

North
Sea

Norway

Sweden   Finland

Baltic
Sea

British Isles

Denmark

Russia

E U R O P E

Alps

River Danube

Black Sea

Portugal

Spain

Mediterranean Sea

0   500 miles
0   500 kilometres

Key
evergreen forest
mountains
tundra
borderlines

The rest of Europe has a temperate **climate**.
This means that it is not too hot or too cold.

A thousand years ago, forests covered almost all
of Europe. Since then most of the forests have
been cut down, and the land is now farmed.
Forests, tundra, and scrub are different types of
habitat. A habitat includes all the plants that grow
in an area and all the wild animals that live there.

Rosemary

Rosemary grows well in the scrub-land around the Mediterranean Sea. It is very dry here in summer, so there are often **wildfires**. Rosemary contains an oil that makes it burn quickly in a wildfire. Amazingly, this helps the plant to survive. The wood and leaves burn so fast that the fire passes before it can damage the plant's roots. New growth quickly sprouts up again.

Rosemary grows wild in the countries around the Mediterranean Sea.

Plant oils

Several plants have oils that give their leaves a particular smell and flavour. Rosemary leaves are used in cooking, especially to flavour lamb.

Saving water

The oil found in the rosemary plant also helps it save water. When the sun is hot, gases from the oils hang in the air above the plant. They act like a blanket and stop water escaping from the leaves. The leaves are shaped like small needles. Very little water escapes from them because they have a small **surface area**.

ROSEMARY

HEIGHT:
UP TO 2 METRES
(6.5 FEET)

LIFESPAN:
MANY YEARS

HABITAT:
MEDITERRANEAN
SCRUB

THAT'S AMAZING!
ROSEMARY OIL IS USED IN HAIR LOTIONS, SKIN CREAMS, AND TO FLAVOUR AN ALCOHOLIC DRINK CALLED VERMOUTH.

where wild rosemary is found

North Sea

Atlantic Ocean

Europe

Mediterranean Sea

Rosemary has tough, leathery leaves. They contain a smelly oil.

Cork oak

Cork oaks grow near the western end of the Mediterranean Sea. Most of the cork stoppers in the world come from the **bark** of these trees. Cork is used for stoppers because it is waterproof. Cork is made up of tiny pockets filled with air. They protect the tree during a wildfire. Although some of the bark burns, the air pockets stop the heat reaching deep inside the trunk of the tree.

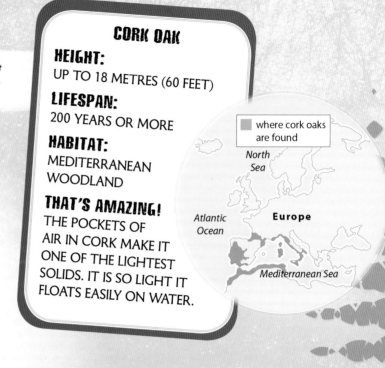

CORK OAK

HEIGHT:
UP TO 18 METRES (60 FEET)

LIFESPAN:
200 YEARS OR MORE

HABITAT:
MEDITERRANEAN WOODLAND

THAT'S AMAZING!
THE POCKETS OF AIR IN CORK MAKE IT ONE OF THE LIGHTEST SOLIDS. IT IS SO LIGHT IT FLOATS EASILY ON WATER.

where cork oaks are found

North Sea

Atlantic Ocean

Europe

Mediterranean Sea

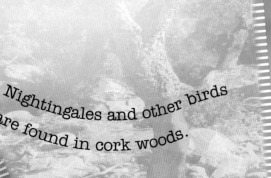

Nightingales and other birds are found in cork woods.

Cork is gathered by stripping the bark off a cork oak.

Harvest time

It takes about 25 years for a cork oak to grow big enough for its bark to be harvested. After that the cork bark can be peeled off without damaging the tree. The cork grows back, and can be peeled off again every nine years. Cork oaks are grown just for their cork. Today, people are using plastic stoppers or screw caps instead of corks because they are easier to make.

Foxglove

Every part of this plant contains a **poison** called digitalis. People who eat foxgloves, especially the leaves, can die. Even so, tiny amounts of digitalis are used to make a medicine that saves people's lives. The medicine makes the heart work better.

FOXGLOVE

HEIGHT:
UP TO 1.5 METRES
(5 FEET)

LIFESPAN:
ABOUT 15 MONTHS

HABITAT:
OPEN WOODS, HEATHS,
MOUNTAINS

THAT'S AMAZING!
FOXGLOVE LEAVES USED TO
BE MADE INTO A HERBAL TEA
TO CURE SORE THROATS.
HOWEVER, PEOPLE DIED FROM
DRINKING TOO MUCH OF IT!

where foxgloves are found

North Sea

Atlantic Ocean

Europe

Mediterranean Sea

A foxglove has up to 80 flowers on its long stalk. Each flower is shaped like the finger of a glove.

Seed to plant

Foxglove **seeds** often sprout on land that has been dug up. The **seedlings** grow quickly on the cleared ground, but the plant does not produce a flower until the following year.

Inside the flower

The inside of the flower is spotted with deep purple. Bees follow the purple spots to the **pollen** in the centre of the flower. Once the flower has made seeds, the plant dies.

Be careful! Foxgloves are poisonous, so do not touch them.

Pollen

Pollen is yellow dust. A flower uses pollen from other flowers to make seeds. Ripe seeds grow into new plants.

Bracken

Bracken is a type of fern. It grows best on open hillsides and in woods where the trees have been cut down.

Poisonous plant

Bracken spreads quickly because it is poisonous. Animals do not eat it unless there are no other plants to graze on. The poison does not kill immediately, but it causes cancer, a disease that develops slowly.

Deer and other animals know that bracken is poisonous to eat.

Ferns

A fern's leaves are called fronds. New fronds unroll from the tip of the stem. Its seeds are tiny **spores** that blow in the wind.

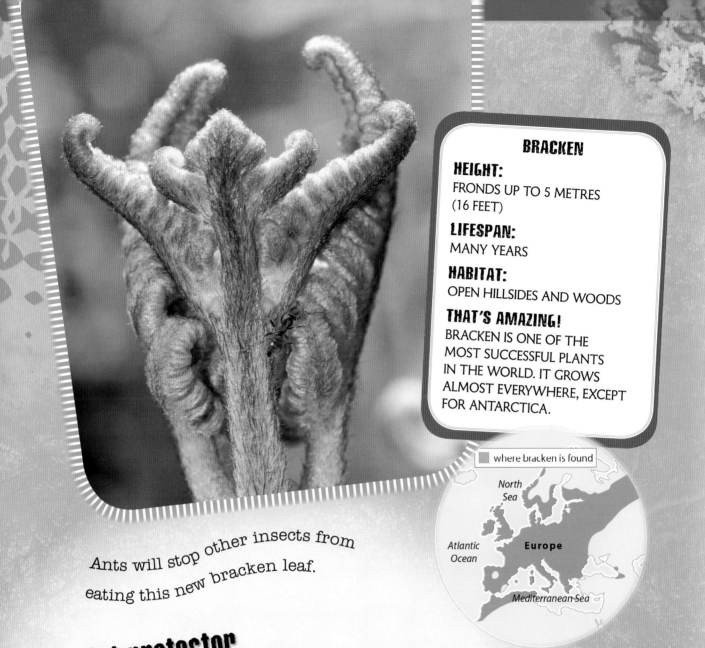

BRACKEN

HEIGHT:
FRONDS UP TO 5 METRES
(16 FEET)

LIFESPAN:
MANY YEARS

HABITAT:
OPEN HILLSIDES AND WOODS

THAT'S AMAZING!
BRACKEN IS ONE OF THE
MOST SUCCESSFUL PLANTS
IN THE WORLD. IT GROWS
ALMOST EVERYWHERE, EXCEPT
FOR ANTARCTICA.

North
Sea

Atlantic
Ocean

Europe

Mediterranean Sea

Ants will stop other insects from eating this new bracken leaf.

Ant protector

The young leaves, or fronds, of bracken
are not poisonous and people sometimes
eat them. The plant has a special way of
stopping insects eating the new fronds. It
produces a sweet juice near the tip of the
new frond. The juice attracts ants, which
then chase away all other insects!

Glacial buttercup

Glacial buttercups grow in the Arctic and near the tops of high mountains. They grow close to huge masses of ice, called glaciers. Glacial buttercups are one of the few plants that can grow so close to a glacier. As the edges of the ice melt in summer, the plants use the melted water to quickly grow leaves.

A glacial buttercup has a strong stem and fat, glossy leaves.

Reindeer food

There is very little soil so close to the ice. Glacial buttercups grow in small pockets of soil in damp cracks in the rocks. The flowers are shining white when they first open, but soon they turn pink and then purple. Reindeer also live high in the mountains during summer. They love to eat these buttercups!

Glaciers are getting smaller. As they melt they leave behind gravel. The gravel mixes with dead moss and **lichens** to make soil.

GLACIAL BUTTERCUP

HEIGHT:
FLOWER STEMS UP TO 15 CENTIMETRES (6 INCHES)

LIFESPAN:
USUALLY LESS THAN 5 YEARS

HABITAT:
SNOWY MOUNTAIN TOPS

THAT'S AMAZING!
IN EUROPE GLACIAL BUTTERCUPS GROW HIGHER UP MOUNTAINS THAN ANY OTHER FLOWER.

North Sea

Atlantic Ocean

Europe

☐ where glacial buttercups are found

Scurvy-grass

North Sea

Atlantic Ocean

Europe

where scurvy grass is found

Scurvy-grass grows along the coast, where it is often splashed by sea water. The salt in sea water would kill most plants, but scurvy-grass has leathery leaves that keep salt water out. Scurvy-grass cannot use the salt water in the soil. It has to wait until it rains heavily. Then its leaves take in and store fresh water.

Scurvy-grass is common on rocky coasts all around Europe.

Medicine plant

Sailors used to eat scurvy-grass to protect themselves from a disease called scurvy. That's how the plant got its name! Scurvy causes bleeding inside the body. People get scurvy when they eat no fruit or vegetables for several months. In the past, sailors ate scurvy-grass because they could not get enough fresh fruit during long sea journeys.

Scurvy-grass has small, white flowers and thick, tough leaves.

Vitamin C

The leaves and fruit of scurvy-grass contain vitamin C. This is one of the many **nutrients** people need to stay healthy.

Glasswort

Glasswort grows on **salt marshes**. The land here is covered by sea water twice a day when the level of the sea rises. The rising and falling level of the sea is called the tide. The salt in sea water kills most plants, but glasswort has a tough skin that keeps the salt out.

Glasswort is one of the few plants that can grow in the salty soil of a salt marsh.

GLASSWORT

HEIGHT:
UP TO 30 CENTIMETRES
(12 INCHES)

LIFESPAN:
LESS THAN A YEAR

HABITAT:
SALT MARSHES

THAT'S AMAZING!
WHEN GLASSWORT
IS BURNED, THE ASH
CAN BE MIXED WITH
SAND TO MAKE A ROUGH
KIND OF GLASS. NO ONE KNOWS
WHO MADE THIS DISCOVERY
HUNDREDS OF YEARS AGO.

North Sea

Atlantic Ocean

Europe

Mediterranean Sea

where glasswort is found

Glasswort stores fresh water in its stem, in the same way that a desert cactus does.

Storing water

The sea water makes the soil very salty. Like other plants, glasswort needs to take in fresh rainwater through its roots. It can only do this when it rains heavily and the **marsh** is not covered by sea water. Then the plant takes in fresh water and stores it in its stem.

Roots

Roots anchor a plant in the soil. They take in water and other nutrients from the soil.

Bladderwort

Bladderwort floats on ponds that contain very few of the nutrients that plants need to survive. To get nutrients, bladderwort traps insects and eats them! It has long, thin leaves with swollen pods, called **bladders.** The leaves float just below the surface of the water. When an insect touches the door of the bladder it springs open, sucking the insect inside. Juices in the bladder slowly break down the insect, then the plant takes in its nutrients.

Bladderwort uses bladders on its underwater leaves to trap insects and other tiny water animals.

insect

Pond flower

The bladderwort's flower is bright yellow but
the plant does not usually flower every year.
In autumn the underwater leaves die back,
and part of the stem falls into the mud at the
bottom of the pond. The next spring the stem
produces new leaves that float up to the
surface of the pond.

The bladderwort's flower grows from the stem and above the surface of the water.

BLADDERWORT

HEIGHT:
STEMS UP TO 1 METRE
(40 INCHES)

LIFESPAN:
SEVERAL YEARS

HABITAT:
PONDS, LAKES, AND DITCHES

THAT'S AMAZING!
THE BLADDERWORT'S
TRAPDOOR SPRINGS SHUT
IN JUST 1/35TH OF A SECOND.
THIS IS TOO FAST FOR ANY
INSECT TO ESCAPE!

North
Sea

Atlantic
Ocean

Europe

where bladderwort
is found

Rootless duckweed

Duckweeds are the smallest flowering plants in the world. They float on the surface of ponds and ditches. They are so small they can even grow in a cow's muddy footprint!

No roots

A duckweed has one tiny leaf which is also the plant's stem. Most duckweeds have a root that dangles below this leaf, but rootless duckweed does not.

Rootless duckweed is the smallest duckweed. It is even smaller than the eye of a needle.

No flowers

Rootless duckweed does not even have a flower. Like all duckweeds, it produces new plants by budding. A small "daughter" plant grows on the side of the duckweed, then splits off and floats away. This way of producing new plants works so well that duckweed can quickly cover a whole pond.

ROOTLESS DUCKWEED

HEIGHT:
LESS THAN 1 MILLIMETRE (1/25 INCH)

LIFESPAN:
LESS THAN A YEAR

HABITAT:
PONDS AND DITCHES

THAT'S AMAZING!
DUCKWEEDS SPREAD EASILY FROM ONE PLACE TO ANOTHER. IN THE UNITED STATES, DUCKWEEDS HAVE BEEN FOUND IN MELTING HAILSTONES. THEY MIGHT HAVE BEEN SUCKED UP INTO THE CLOUDS BY A TORNADO.

where rootless duckweed is found

North Sea

Atlantic Ocean

Europe

Mediterranean Sea

Ducks and other water birds feed on duckweed.

Reindeer moss

Reindeer moss is not a moss. It is not even a proper plant. It is a lichen.

Photosynthesis

Green plants make sugar in their leaves. They combine water from the soil with carbon dioxide gas from the air. To do this, they use the energy of sunlight. The process is called photosynthesis.

Tough plant

Lichens are the toughest living things in the world. They can survive in the Arctic where it is too cold for green plants. The body of the lichen is a **fungus**. It takes in water from rain, but it cannot make food. Instead, the fungus shelters an **alga**. The alga makes food for both the fungus and the alga using **photosynthesis** (see box).

Reindeer moss grows on the Arctic tundra.

REINDEER MOSS

HEIGHT:
UP TO 8 CENTIMETRES (3 INCHES)

LIFESPAN:
40 YEARS OR MORE

HABITAT:
TUNDRA AND MOUNTAINS

THAT'S AMAZING!
REINDEER MOSS GROWS LESS THAN 5 MILLIMETRES (1/5 INCH) A YEAR. THIS IS SLOWER THAN YOUR FINGERNAILS!

North Sea

Atlantic Ocean

Europe

where reindeer moss is found

Reindeer, lemmings, and other Arctic animals feed on reindeer moss.

Mountain living

Reindeer moss covers high mountainsides and tundra, where grass cannot grow. Reindeer rely on reindeer moss for food. In winter, they dig in the snow with their hooves or antlers to reach the lichen.

Rosewarne Learning Centre

Plants in danger

Some types of plant are in danger of becoming **extinct** in the wild. There are so few of these plants that soon there may be none left at all. They are said to be endangered.

Why plants become endangered

Plants become endangered for different reasons. For example, yellow marsh saxifrage grows in marshes on hillsides. Farmers have drained many of these marshes, so there is nowhere for the flowers to grow.

Yellow marsh saxifrage is now so rare that it is protected by law.

The lady's slipper orchid is one of the most beautiful orchids. People have picked so many of them that the plant has become endangered. At one time there was only one plant left growing in Britain! Since then, scientists have managed to grow new plants from seeds. They have planted the seeds in the wild. The places where the flowers are now growing are carefully protected.

Lady's slipper orchid is one of the rarest flowers in Europe.

Plant facts and figures

There are millions of different kinds of plants growing all over the world. The place where a plant lives is called its habitat. Plants have special features, such as flowers, leaves, and stems. These features allow plants to survive in their habitats. Which plant do you think is the most amazing?

ROSEMARY

HEIGHT:
UP TO 2 METRES (6.5 FEET)

LIFESPAN:
MANY YEARS

HABITAT:
MEDITERRANEAN SCRUB

THAT'S AMAZING!
ROSEMARY OIL IS USED IN HAIR LOTIONS, SKIN CREAMS, AND TO FLAVOUR AN ALCOHOLIC DRINK CALLED VERMOUTH.

CORK OAK

HEIGHT:
UP TO 18 METRES (60 FEET)

LIFESPAN:
200 YEARS OR MORE

HABITAT:
MEDITERRANEAN WOODLAND

THAT'S AMAZING!
THE POCKETS OF AIR IN CORK MAKE IT ONE OF THE LIGHTEST SOLIDS. IT IS SO LIGHT IT FLOATS EASILY ON WATER.

FOXGLOVE

HEIGHT:
UP TO 1.5 METRES (5 FEET)

LIFESPAN:
ABOUT 15 MONTHS

HABITAT:
OPEN WOODS, HEATHS, MOUNTAINS

THAT'S AMAZING!
FOXGLOVE LEAVES USED TO BE MADE INTO A HERBAL TEA TO CURE SORE THROATS. HOWEVER, PEOPLE DIED FROM DRINKING TOO MUCH OF IT!

BRACKEN

HEIGHT:
FRONDS UP TO 5 METRES (16 FEET)

LIFESPAN:
MANY YEARS

HABITAT:
OPEN HILLSIDES AND WOODS

THAT'S AMAZING!
BRACKEN IS ONE OF THE MOST SUCCESSFUL PLANTS IN THE WORLD. IT GROWS ALMOST EVERYWHERE, EXCEPT FOR ANTARCTICA.

GLACIAL BUTTERCUP

HEIGHT:
FLOWER STEMS UP TO
15 CENTIMETRES (6 INCHES)

LIFESPAN:
USUALLY LESS THAN
5 YEARS

HABITAT:
SNOWY MOUNTAIN TOPS

THAT'S AMAZING!
IN EUROPE GLACIAL
BUTTERCUPS GROW
HIGHER UP MOUNTAINS
THAN ANY
OTHER FLOWER.

SCURVY-GRASS

HEIGHT:
STEMS CAN BE MORE
THAN 50 CENTIMETRES
(20 INCHES)

LIFESPAN:
2–5 YEARS

HABITAT:
ROCKY SEA COASTS

THAT'S AMAZING!
IN SPITE OF ITS NAME,
SCURVY-GRASS IS NOT
A GRASS BUT A TYPE
OF CRESS. IN THE PAST
PEOPLE ATE SCURVY-
GRASS SANDWICHES!

GLASSWORT

HEIGHT:
UP TO 30 CENTIMETRES
(12 INCHES)

LIFESPAN:
LESS THAN A YEAR

HABITAT:
SALT MARSHES

THAT'S AMAZING!
WHEN GLASSWORT IS
BURNED, THE ASH CAN
BE MIXED WITH SAND
TO MAKE A ROUGH
KIND OF GLASS. NO ONE
KNOWS WHO MADE THIS
DISCOVERY HUNDREDS
OF YEARS AGO.

BLADDERWORT

HEIGHT:
STEMS UP TO 1 METRE
(40 INCHES)

LIFESPAN:
SEVERAL YEARS

HABITAT:
PONDS, LAKES, AND
DITCHES

THAT'S AMAZING!
THE BLADDERWORT'S
TRAPDOOR SPRINGS
SHUT IN JUST 1/35TH
OF A SECOND. THIS IS
TOO FAST FOR ANY
INSECT TO ESCAPE!

ROOTLESS DUCKWEED

HEIGHT:
LESS THAN 1 MILLIMETRE
(1/25 INCH)

LIFESPAN:
LESS THAN A YEAR

HABITAT:
PONDS AND DITCHES

THAT'S AMAZING!
DUCKWEEDS SPREAD
EASILY FROM ONE PLACE
TO ANOTHER. IN THE
UNITED STATES
DUCKWEEDS HAVE BEEN
FOUND IN MELTING
HAILSTONES. THEY MIGHT
HAVE BEEN SUCKED UP
INTO THE CLOUDS BY
A TORNADO.

REINDEER MOSS

HEIGHT:
UP TO 8 CENTIMETRES
(3 INCHES)

LIFESPAN:
40 YEARS OR MORE

HABITAT:
TUNDRA AND
MOUNTAINS

THAT'S AMAZING!
REINDEER MOSS GROWS
LESS THAN 5 MILLIMETRES
(1/5 INCH) A YEAR.
THIS IS SLOWER THAN
YOUR FINGERNAILS!

Find out more

Books to read

Animals and Plants, Andrew Langley (Oxford University Press, 2002)

Plant Life Cycles, Anita Ganeri (Heinemann Library, 2006)

Plants and Planteaters (Secrets of the Rainforest), Michael Chinery (Crabtree Publishing Company, 2000)

Plants and the Environment, Jennifer Boothroyd (Lerner Publishing Group, 2007)

Plants that Eat Animals, Allan Fowler (Children's Press, 2001)

The Power of Plants, Claire Lewellyn (Oxford University Press, 2005)

The World's Largest Plants, Susan Blackaby (Picture Window Books, 2005)

Websites

www.kidsgeo.com/geography-for-kids/0153-biosphere.php
Learn more about weather, habitats, and how plants survive in them.

www.mbgnet.net/bioplants/adapt.html
Discover how plants adapt to different habitats, including deserts, grasslands, tropical rainforests, temperate forests, tundra, and water.

www.plantcultures.org/
Find out about plants from all over the world at Kew Gardens' website.

Glossary

alga simple form of living thing. It has no roots or flowers, but it can make its own food by photosynthesis.

Arctic area surrounding the North Pole

bark hard outer layer of wood that covers the trunk and branches of a tree

bladder soft, hollow bag

climate type of weather a place usually has

extinct no longer in existence

fungus one of a group of living things that feed on other living or dead things

habitat place in the wild where particular types of plant grow and particular types of animal live

lichen living thing that consists of a fungus and an alga living closely together

marsh land that is partly covered by shallow water

nutrient part of food that is needed for health

photosynthesis process by which plants make their own food using the energy of sunlight

poison something harmful if eaten or touched

pollen yellow dust made by flowers

salt marsh land that is sometimes covered by seawater, for example twice a day at high tide

seed part of a plant that can grow into a new plant

seedling young plant

spore seed made by ferns, mosses, and fungi

surface area the area of the surface of an object, such as a leaf

tundra land near the North and South Poles where it is too cold for trees to grow

wildfire fire that starts by accident in the wild and is difficult to put out

Index